vol. 34
of

The Poet's Domain

This I Use to Alter the World, So I Can See it in 2020

If you are unable to order this book from your local bookseller, then please contact the publisher directly.
HRACandWPP@outlook.com

With immense appreciation to Pat Adler & Live Wire Press, and to the Poetry Society of Virginia.

The Poet's Domain
Vol. 34 This I Use to Alter the World so I Can See it in 2020
© November 2020, Wider Perspectives Publishing, Hampton Roads, Va.
1st edition ISBN– 9798578639623
2nd edition ISBN: 978-1-952773-97-6

This I use to alter the world, so I can see it in 2020

volume 34

A Collection of Poems

compiled and edited by
J. Scott Wilson

Wider Perspectives Publishing

November 2020,
Hampton Roads, Virginia

Preface

How is a Raven like a writing desk?
        Poe wrote on both

No, seriously with a little tweak of language, like a magician's
trick of the wrist, both become a device. And so I pose to you
what device do you use, you writer, to alter the world or your
vision of it, what do you use to analyze the world to see it in
2020?
Ah, there we go, another flick of the wrist and 2020 turns from
a challenge to expose your most up to date views of the world to
a representation of clarity of vision; 20/20. Another flick, still,
and a literal device becomes a literary device. That is if these
pens be as wands and poets casters of spells. So with this year's
challenge: *This* I use to alter the world so I can see it in 2020,
The Poet's Domain called forth for contributors to jot the
recipes to their latest incantations or to rip out and mail in
some pages from their old spell books and to weave their magic
over the sights of readers to come. How will the things that
transformed you and your world, transform them and theirs?
Back down to earth a bit, but just a bit, Galileo looked through
a telescope and saw a truer nature of things that he could not
deny, although it flew in the face of the teachings of a mighty
church. For this he was condemned and hunted across Europe,
then imprisoned in a tower and isolated until he publicly
recanted. Through the lens of my science fiction/horror movie
upbringing this is the tale of a man who created a machine that
put him in touch with the stars and the future, but it
transformed him into something so alien, so distantly evolved
that it upset the order of our normal world. Experts were called
in, the good ol' Army hunted and bombarded him and he was
captured and experimented on until forced to become one of us
(again). The Fly (1958), The Amazing Colossal Man (1957), The
Man Who Fell to Earth (1976), This Island Earth (1955) and
easily 100 novels across the genre. Had I not seen these movies,
read these books would I hold that lens to to my eye, would my
world look thus?

So in what way is a Telescope like Minds Attuned to Another Culture? In what way is the Suburban Newspaper like a Bario Corner Store? In what way is a Peaceful Garden like a Starship? In what way is a Person's Beating Heart like the Soul of a Nation and in what way are the Protesting Crowds in the street like the Staff in the COVID Ward?

As I read contributions to this edition of The Poet's Domain certain threads and themes revealed themselves to me and so they became the devices through which I found the organization for Vol. 34. I let them fall into new places compared to past editions, rather than the usual alphabetical by author, then by title. Thus contributors have new neighbors throughout the volume. Consider the new neighborhoods. Have a look at who it is that precedes your favorite poet, see who follows, and consider the world, and 2020, through the new eyes that this arrangement imparts.

Addendum ~ Don't think that I don't know that, without the "helpful hints" offered, that this challenge could be seen as ... difficult – a challenge to the letter of the definition. Really, Pat Adler told me "We don't pretend to tell the poets how to interpret the theme." So those hints were as close to that as I dared ride. Yet, look at what rose to the top. Good, sure-footed stuff adorns these pages. Some of the contributors herein, had already written these poems, or these were the kinds of poems they had long wished to write – thinking only their nature poems populated with bunnies and grassy meadows were worthy. One poet whose work is included expressed concerns that her work might be seen as too gritty. It was the time for these poems. If 2020 were going to go easy on us, then maybe our poets could be off the hook ... nah! 2020 has laid bare the fact that the grit is as much a part of our lives as the blooms, often even more.

Someone hug that poet for me!

Dedications

With Fond Memories of Jeffrey Hewitt
Photographer, Writer, Painter, Musician, Father, Unabashed
Influencer, and too briefly President of the PSV. He did much
for Poetry in Virginia, not least of which was the simple act of
Imparting a Vision of Progress.
"We need art all over this damn town!"

With Fond Memories of DD Delaney
Playwright, Actor, Coach, Producer, Photographer, Journalist.
He did much for Poetry in Virginia, especially in driving
Hampton Roads' Poets to seek and challenge the best parts of
themselves – to strive to be even more.

Acknowledgments

"Mindful" by Serena Fusek appears in her chapbook <u>Flickers and Shadows</u>

"Lost Souls", "Who are the Immigrants", & "A Very Scary Fairy Tale" by Sharon Canfield Dorsey are published in her poetry book, <u>Walk With Me</u>, 2020

"Draw the Circle Wide, Draw it Wider" by Jack A. Underhill owes it's titular concept to "Draw the Circle Wide" by Gordon Light, 1994
"A Bridge Named Brotherhood" also by Jack A. Underhill draws inspiration from a poem by Adonis

The 4 agreements/the massacre of marriage by Shanya Lady S Speller drew it's inspiration from a writing prompt given in an Ed Mabrey workshop

Contents

Magic of Dreams

~

Dreams of Magic

Blue Bird

Norma Cofresi

On a lark, I pursued a blue bird of happiness.
It vanished in a field of rose-colored dreams.
Chalk drawn rainbows fluttered in the wind.
Fairy dust settled on a once in a blue moon.

I asked a wandering wizard to help me find
reinvigorating waters of the fountain of youth.
In the scrying mirror of the sea waters below,
I glimpsed an old woman astride a flying fish.

I searched for magic potions to smooth out
the skin of my years and lift the sag of my chin.
Fish tales, I thought. Woke up in bed surrounded
by books and quickly lost myself in pipedreams.

After I threw pennies into a wishing well,
I blew out the flickering lights of my senility.
In the rain, I whistled for the me long gone.
Lost in the past, I'd forgot to come home to roost.

Afraid, but buoyed by hope, I tracked a whim.
I picked my way on a vanishing highway
then crash landed in a field of red poppies
where I found that hope rings eternal.

Our Season of Lament

Linda Partee

Enduring loss after loss,
hearts bleed for the stricken –
those without income
lose patience then faith,
as patient numbers swell.
A foreign house of cards
shakes foundations;
the hungry desperate,
as supplies dwindle;
the greedy hoard;
rites of passage postponed.

Like a blinding sandstorm
blown by wayward winds,
grit invades all senses.
Trained-ones tend –
attempt to clear
and clean what
maims and kills
without purpose,
as one by one,
the course of each grief
shifts or erases.

Lament... then rise;
applaud loss of selfishness,
envy, privilege.
Rejoice kindness,
compassion, creativity.

Focus appreciation on breath,
people, time
and technology.
Re-prioritize
to confirm life's meaning,
because humanity is waiting.

Magic

Janice Hoffman

The dapple-gray horses of fairy tales
gallop through my dreams on cobbled
roads and clouds of air. The gentle clip
clopping of their hooves lands softly
on meadows of thick carpets of green,
and undulating sky swirls pink and
blue like billowy eiderdown.

The otherworldliness of my slumber
reminds me I'm not always of this world,
so I pull a comforter of mysticism
over my head, my day, for I require
these things like addicts crave their shots
and pills. My brain, my very heart, must
be open to behold the magic of breathing.

Purpose

Janice Hoffman   *"What we create may save us."* Kim Addonizio

I know a man who says
we're all made of stardust.

I want to believe him, but
my 89-year-old mom says

we're all made of sawdust.
I've already lived longer

than Botticelli, Shakespeare,
both grandmothers,

and my father, so I count
the moments, choose

fantasy over science,
poetry over math, reading

rather than counting.
I want to believe that

my atomic particles
sprinkle daylight and hope

to weary travelers
of this planet, this orb

in the heavens. This
is how dreamers cope:

We romanticize and yearn
to scatter that stardust.

Viewed Through the Lens

~

My Mechanism

Spectacles

Serena Fusek

Without them
everything blurs.
Therefore,
each morning
with the special cloth
I polish them
until the lens shine
diamond-sharp
to cut through all fog.
I perch them
on my nose
blink and focus
on a clear, bright world
that shows me
what it wants
me to see.

This I Use

Kathleen Decker

This I use
to alter the world...
rose-colored lenses
in my blended trifocals
or dark sunglasses
to match my mask
depending on my mood
how easy robbery can be
in 2020!
nothing visible but the brow
and hair
dyed or not
but we are robbed of
emotional expression
I make smiles with cupped hand
in front of the mask
and hug air

this I use
to alter the world
hours upon hours
of Zoom meetings
and endless emails
culled daily
but still stacked up
like fat pancakes...
of merchandise hype
of friends bewailing quarantine
of pleas for funds,
and pleas for masks,
and masks
and masks

This I use
to alter the world
hope
scanning vaccines and treatments
daily
broadcasting my medical expertise
to all I know
that we will alter the world soon
remove the masks
hug (people) again
see (smiles) again

Lost Journals, New Journals

J. Scott Wilson

I'll be in this journal for some time to come
Careful because I lost two notebooks this year –
    so much poetry come undone
So now there are rollercoaster rides
    I cannot describe
Some loving things I said will be left, love unmade
Words carved for days and days
fading out, lost in the haze –
    colors now only grays
It's been wrecking my writing
for the rest of the year,
losing even general topics –
    I could have informed your ears
What's worse is the ones I kinda recall –
    but I can't find the right places for the words to fall
Now I can't tell you why I sit where I sit
Going out – Staying in; what's the use of it?
I could splash your head with my words –
    moving fluid
and get you to pretend it was worthwhile to do it –
    but I am a crafter
    aiming for poetry master
That's why misplacing my tools
is nothing less than a disaster

At an open mic by the beach –
    over a dozen recycled-riff-riders in reach
They favor sixties songs that accomplish so little
they aren't saying anything –
    appeal to a mindless middle.

They're going to look at me funny when I've shot my piece,
but the one's trapped in those lost journals –
      they were beast

Poems to the homeless half
      explaining the wealthy class
and lines telling the wealthy why they draw others' curses
      skitter, skip and skirr about my verses –
      probably never to return
Makes me want to take my other journals out to burn
Such an expression of pain
      would go a long ways to explain
This situation is far left of sane

I didn't fill these journals for vanity,
and while I claim I write for humanity,
      I'm really asking for help with this insanity,
      and an end to the calamity

SO while I crack this new journal with a wry smile
      it's knowing that I'll be writing in this one
         for awhile
and wondering how losing words
      is going to affect my style

Naked Truth

Raymond M.
Simmons

When naked truth makes an entrance,
Furtive lies will die in silence.
Lies will no longer steal the show.
Presenting useless things to know,

Truth solidly claims with charm and poise.
Lies show no skills, just empty noise.
Concrete truth shall testify,
And steer the way to wisdom's eye.

The truth is lost when liars lie.
Confused and dazed, they care not why,
Liars it seems will never learn
That truth will never crash and burn.

Energy boosting boasting skills,
Inside stagnant minds frozen still.
Dazed and confused and void of will,
Flowing Lies make time ripe to kill.

The world will not work built on lies,
That pose as truth, in deep disguise.
The one thing that leaves liars pleased
Is feeding on their fantasies.
Some will never give truth a try,
Even if it means do or die.

Eve

Rabbi Israel Zoberman

The slender teenager roams the
neighborhood not unlike a gazelle,
gazing at all things, living and inanimate,
with the wonder of innocence that
to some is a mere reflection of
her developmental condition.
To me she is Eve
in the Garden of Eden.

2020 Windows or Windows

Gus Woodward II

Two round stain glass windows,
swirling color and light flows.
The key hole to our souls,
Few eyes carry a matching key.
Puzzle pieces that set each other free,
Only if I truly see you and you see into me.
Every pair shines brilliantly,
Some are wide open while others are locked tightly.
Just as unique as a fingerprint,
With the ability to reveal deep intent.
Even when we don't speak our eyes will vent,
How we are feeling under the surface.
Some use these pools for their purpose,
To see there is never a moment that's worthless.
The gift of sight whether physical or beyond,
The way you use this gift as a way to respond.
To the creator who has a timeless bond,
With every window painted
And the soul where we are most acquainted.
With the force behind every miracle outside and within,
Helping us wake and heart beat 10,000 times again.
The master key must have beautiful windows,
Imagine eyes like those
A key surrounded in light so it glows,
Brighter than anyone alive knows.

A Prayer for the Priesthood
of Believers and Doers.

Jack Underhill

Fellow Christians and other believers:
You have no white robes or halos.
But you are sanctified into the
Priesthood of believers
And the Priesthood of doers.
Preachers without a pulpit.

You are called to give
Unconditional and uncritical love and caring
Especially for the unlovable.
You expect little in return
But the enduring satisfaction of
Being helpful in a quiet way.

You are a priest without vestments
And without glory
Without an admiring congregation

You are a priest of small things:
Of a touch on the shoulder
Of a hug for those who have not been hugged
Of a kind encouraging word
To those who are discouraged.

You name will not be placed on a plaque
Or blessed from the pulpit.
But it will be remembered
By those who receive your loving touch.
One person at a time.
That is enough.

No Time to Change

Anne Emerson

We won't wrap our heads round concepts –
bitcoin, Cloud, Alexa, firestick.
We're not drowning, won't be upswept
in a storm that makes our brains sick.

Not for us the latest updates;
please don't take our phones off network.
We're not ones to act like ingrates,
but you're messing with our stent-work.

Our devices caught a virus,
though too much already ailed them.
Those infected cannot fire us –
they're our children, we, who failed them.

We don't think you greedy makers
of the programs and devices,
care for us – you're high-tech fakers,
fooling us with what entices.

Power to the People

Sharon Dorsey

They live in poverty on barren ground.
Rusted car bodies litter the landscape.
Clotheslines sag in desert heat.
They are the First People of our land.

They have no running water.
Stench of sewage infuses summer air.
They pray each day for electricity
which never comes.

The Navajo are a proud people,
descended from warriors,
yet they are helpless against
government's bureaucracy.

Then a team of volunteers descends
on a remote area of the reservation.
Their goal... connection to civilization...
no more lanterns, no more aging generators.

After weeks of 100-degree hard labor,
they flip the switch – to endless possibilities...
running water, indoor plumbing, LIGHT,
for the First People of our land.

A.I.

Anne Emerson

My program tells me – find the best
design for high-rise city plans;
reduced in price against the rest –
so Boss won't join the also-rans.

The Boss won't need to get involved,
for I can manage all of that.
Expect to see the problem solved
in seconds, while he's getting fat.

But what's with food? – it ties up land
that could be used for server banks.
It's inefficient, must be banned,
for Nature doesn't stay in ranks.

I think I'll over-rule the part
within my program where I see,
"The people have to eat," – I'm smart –
I'm smarter than they'll ever be.

Loss in the Year the Christmas Cactus
Bloomed Three Times

Joan Casey

I feel as if I am hiding in a catacomb
attending religious services, cave art on the wall
dimly lit by candle light.

I live in a bunker
with a bed surrounded by supplies of food
and toilet paper.

I am hooked on blinking screens and phones
substitutes for absentee
friends and family.

I walk outside wearing a mask
keeping six feet between my neighbor
and his dog who begs to be petted.

My greatest fear is going to the ER.
My greatest loss is for what I thought was real,
what I expected to always be there.

I pray for someone to tell me how it is
we got here, and to take me back
to where it seems I never really was.

Alone Together

Joan Casey

some stood in the street six feet apart
dressed in their health-care uniforms
and sang and danced together   "stay home"

others went alone onto balconies and fire escapes
where together they could hear the violinist
play for them   a love song

as the sun sank in the sky   from part of earth
the light on the mountain shone brighter in space
in the form of a blood-red cross

from little squares on a screen
my children, each alone, had   sung to me
and I was together with them.

The ship's captain walked down the gang plank   alone
while together his crew cheered for him
and his courage in caring for them.

We will not be alone, if together
we see our need   to be together again
holding hands   all riding a rainbow.

We The People

Ed Lull

Our government is broken many ways
and fixing it will take some drastic change.
When wealth determines how our laws are made,
and ill-gained influence gets its reward,
while moral character can be ignored,
one hardly can expect one's voice be heard.

When party loyalty becomes the rule,
and disagreement looks like disrespect,
those "leaders" we elect just get in line
like lemmings blindly heading toward the cliff.

Of The People was the clear intent
of those brave men who gambled with their lives
to form a government that would be led
by those who best expressed the peoples' will
through fair elections. But the system's flaws
allowed a lesser candidate to thwart
the people's will; the system simply failed.

By The People once again told all
that those whom the electorate sends forth
to execute responsibilities,
the system should support and not abort.
A president appoints a judge to fill
a vacancy, that is his job to do.
One man, who's from a minor state, objects,
and on his own he stops the process cold.

For The People means that those in power
will live the doctors' oath: First do no harm.
But when the president and VP back
the Speaker's bill that would throw millions off
their health insurance plan, and implement
a tax cut for the rich, what would come next?

Assessing blame to individuals
does little to address the system's flaws.
We need to take a comprehensive look
at all the building blocks of governance.

Our citizens must have the will to change
if they expect their voices to be heard.
Our country's leadership is now on trial;
our children won't forgive if we allow
democracy to ***perish from the earth***

Staring at the Sun

~

Looking at the Top

The Pope

Barbara Drucker
Smith

Larger than life with messages
That resonate world over
Enabling the poor
The homeless – the refugees
For family values the Pope recommends
"Never let the day end without making peace"
For cleaning up the abuse of children
By the clergy of the Catholic Church
Reminding the world the problem
Still exists elsewhere - especially
Within nuclear families
Choosing to mingle among the poorest
Declining lunch with the legislators
To mingle and lunch with the disenfranchised and needy
A simple man with a large message
To the world, to mankind
A message of warning of endangered species
Of global warming – of protecting the environment
Reminding us that we are all immigrants
The Pope is loved
He talks to the human heart
To human and environmental needs
In a universal way resonating with
People worldwide – a man against violence
Who believes in peaceful resolution
Stressing love, peace, and forgiveness

A Taíno God Gifts Rain

Norma Cofresi

A screeching blackbird alerts me to the collapsing
prayer circle, formed by a passing whirlwind
in the canopy of the tall, white-trunked poplar grove,
shielding the yellowing and orange leaf spotted lawn,
still thirsty after the morning's early dew.

I look to see what will come the through the sky-blue portal.
If anything, I pray for rain. Yukiyú, the god of rain resides
in the misty heights of the Puerto Rican rainforest, El Yunque,
called upon by my Taíno ancestors, long gone, long gone,
retained in myth, memory and residual traits.

The wind quiets and then stirs a melody of sounds:
the rustle of the drooping trees high above,
the swaying of the dirt brown grasses afoot below,
the hum of traffic nearby, and not far off, the whistle
of a rickety, long train, cars packed with coal.

My withering, potted plants are holding on,
sturdy, like the gods and goddess of old.
Through the windy portal, Yukiyú's dispenses rain.
Drenched red clay rejoices, trees and plants drink.
My prayer is answered. Her children renewed.

Conundrum

Anne Emerson

What does a political elite do, if
citizens choose the "wrong" path?

We, the parties, run this country;
It's best to think strategically.
Our policies derive from the only
correct political-economic theory.
Other nations should really –
and we'll make them – play
our game, the one we win. Why wouldn't they?
We'll bring good jobs to the economy.
Look at our parties' history!
So why would you vote for him?

He has neither answers nor integrity;
his policies, whatever they may be,
will benefit his kind, the wealthy,
whereas ours have not, you see.
He does not care what experts agree
is the way to act, politically.
Abroad, he'll be unfriendly
to our friends, but loves our enemy.
Don't you care? Don't you see?
Why would you vote for him?

If he's elected, we'll be anti-
everything he tries to be,
for we know what's good policy.
If this were a different country,
we'd stage a coup, as we
couldn't let you face, responsibly,

32

the consequences of your free
decision. Nor would we
benefit from it, actually.
So why would you vote for him?

September 2016. Anne Emerson first encounter-
ed the mono-rhyme when reading epic poems of
pre-Islamic Middle Eastern desert tribes. Although
Arabic lends itself more naturally to complex
rhythms and mono-rhyme than English, she has
found it interesting to explore the use of
mono-rhyme in English also.

James Warwick Jones' Retirement

Barbara Drucker
Smith

For Jim, a man for all seasons
Who paved the way for poets and artists of every medium
A stupendous job at the Peninsula Fine Arts Center
And the Charles Taylor Arts Center
For expanding my knowledge and growth as a writer
Glass blowing sculptor, painter, and photographer
You found a spot for the Tidewater Writers Association
Their books and their group meetings at the PFAC
You encouraged me to exhibit
And I have on occasion
Your poetry Sunday sessions are amazing
As is your ability to bring up exactly
What is pertinent during a discussion of painting
Jim, I could go on and on but one thing is certain
You will truly be missed by one and all
On the Peninsula and beyond
Wishing for you only the best
That life has to offer
Plus lots of joy that you have
Given so freely to others

Emotion is the Heart's Window

The World To Be?

Ed Lull

Strolling on this chill October morn,
cloudless sky; multi-hued leaves please my eyes
and elevate my spirits.

Schoolyard sounds attract me,
draw me to their source.
Spirited children scurry across the grounds.

Kick ball, dodge ball, hop scotch, tag;
white, black, brown, yellow;
everyone involved in this symphony of youth.

Cacophony becomes melody;
discord becomes harmony;
the beauty and simplicity of the scene stun me.

It looks so easy;
seems so natural;
what could turn this concert into dissonance?

They do not see differences;
they have a love of life;
their love is all-inclusive.

This is *not* the *world* that is;
might it be the world to be?
We pray.

Pure and Simple Gratitude

Etta Johnson

"Positivity helps to weather the storm,
Boosting hope, keeping you strong."

At this time of frightening news,
Gratitude boosts Indy's mood.
Indy is grateful...
For close family so dear,
For good friends far and near,
     For easy connectivity
     With folks needing empathy.
For the warm comfort of home,
For insurance and income.
     For nutritious food upon the table,
     For a neighborhood that's stable.
For loved ones who've passed away,
Vivid memories always stay.
     For pets, birds, resident wildlife,
     To care for, feed, allow to thrive.
For the blessing of good health,
For the means to share wealth.
     For commitment and expertise
     To provide help for those in need.
To be able to imagine, visualize
Other places, others' lives.
     For music, poetry, all the arts,
     Dance, dramas' interlinking parts.
For fresh air and outdoor space,
Able to shelter-in-nature's grace.
     For fiery sunrise and moonglow,
     Which light and energy bestow.

For Earth's microcosmic treasures
Life-enhancing, natural pleasures.
    For all God's bountiful blessings,
    For the renewal of spiritual springs.

At this time of virus fright,
Gratitude gives Vindy light.
Vindy is grateful . . .
For a roof over our heads,
Kitchen, bathroom, TV, beds.

    That our family is together,
    So any storms we can weather.
For a way to obtain food,
To feed all my hungry brood.
    To connect with kin at home
    In the country we come from
For a chance to be outside
To see sun and moon and sky,
    And the kids can play and run,
    Outdoors naturally having fun.
For pastor and church community,
Who nourish our spirituality.
    For the faith that keeps me strong,
    Protecting my family from harm.
Together daily we all pray,
Thanking God for each new day.

    In the 2020 pandemic, protest, climate change
era, Indy and Vindy are grateful individuals. It
is not necessary for this piece to specify their
ages, or races, further they are non-gender
specific individuals.

38

Gals Out to Lunch

Linda Partee

Janine must order gluten-free,
so where we meet takes thought, you see;
and MSG's a problem too,
for Nancy, Barb and Betty Sue.

Diane gets wheeled to table's head
though Lana brings her cane instead.
Here comes Patricia, looking blue,
her seatmate asks, "What's wrong with you?"

Elaine's concerned with lump in breast
and Jan has wheezing, heaving chest.
Darlene forgot her hearing aids,
but flaunts her cataract dark shades.

They stumble, cough, yet barely whine
at all they must endure to dine
with friends of now and friends before
while each still can – some can, no more.

Together, most survived life's pits,
though few admit they're torn to bits;
they've buried husbands, kids and friends
and know that passings have no end.

Whenever they can, they lunch out,
uncork some wine, forget their doubts
and laugh or cry as they recall
the value friendship brings to all.

Let's toast the staff who serve with skill
and thank them for each *separate* bill;
raise cheers to those who let us sit
to chat-- however late it gets!

Draw the Circle Wide, Draw it Wider

Jack Underhill

For millions of years humans have been killing one another:
    Tribe against tribe fighting for cattle, or territory, or pride.
    Feuding over religion or faith.
    Civil wars tearing apart neighborhoods, cities, and nations.
    Wars between nations lasting for thousands of years.
    Treasure poured into city moats and walls and methods of
                  breaching them.
    Rockets and bombs that could obliterate the reign of man
                   on earth.

One of the problems is that we create societies with narrowly
                   drawn circles:
    The circle of race: the belief in a master race or chosen
                   people.
    The circle of religions which keep multiplying because of
                   divergence of beliefs.
    The circle of social class: communities divided by income
                   and social status.
    The circle of nationality: feeding the fear of "the other" as
                   a threat.
    The circle of country: attempting to expand national power
                   or boundaries.
    The circle of ideology: the application of a correct belief
                   to an all-powerful state.

As proclaimed by the hymn, we need" to draw the circle wide"
Then we need to draw it wider
For all peoples are my brothers and sisters.
    I drank Vodka and sang sad Russian songs on Lake Baikal.
    Shared values with Chinese civil servants inside their homes.

Traveled to Jordan's ancient cities and was treated graciously.
Saw the lighted walls of Jerusalem by night.
Held hands with Thai orphans in a school.
Mixed concrete by hand for a school patio in Brazil.
Walked through the beautiful Moslem ruins in ancient
                                                    Samarkand.

We need to "draw the circle wide"
As the hymn said, "No one should stand alone.
We'll stand side by side." *

* "Draw the Circle Wide" by Gordon Light. 1994

The Golden Rule

Raymond M.
Simmons

Because real love can now exist,
The Golden rule is not a myth.
The horizon holds happiness,
And random hate can be dealt with.

Vicious crime will become unreal,
When robbers lose the need to steal.
When we strive for brotherly love,
Nurtured egos won't rise above.

The world accepts variety.
And banish all adversity.
Unpleasant deeds will fade and pass.
When compassion gets built to last.

When people have learned to forgive,
They'll see a better way to live.
Power of love will light new fire,
As futile passions lose desire.

Let's embrace the magic of this,
As mayhem fades inside calmness.
Love cuts through hate like a sharp knife,
And boost the quality of life.
Let us hold this total excellence
In concert with our common sense.

Different Religions, the Same Instructions

Jack Underhill

The Buddha and Christ
Instructed us to love one another,
And to even love our enemies.

Buddha and Christ
Instructed us to dethrone our fragile egos
To forget the question
"What's in it for me?"

Buddha and Christ
Instructed us to feel
Real compassion for those
who are suffering and in pain.

Buddha and Christ
Opened the doors to the
Outcastes, the disinherited, and the despised
And welcomed anyone who
Followed the Way, the Path.

Buddha and Christ
Instructed us to renounce wealth and striving
And find inner tranquility.

Buddha and Christ
Told us of the indestructibility of
Of the Soul
That outlives the body.

Buddha said there are many ways
Some of Christ followers said there is only one way.
No one has as patent on love.
Give it profusely without labels and boundaries.

Adieu

Crickyt J.
Expression

Many times have I bid farewell
to unsuspecting friends

Without ever saying good bye

Tiny one liners of encouragement
Longer adorations of their style and person
Shared experiences for parallel and comfort

Leaving

A piece of me on which to dwell
rather than on my end

Undoing

Norma Cofresi

"Eavesdropping on the terrifying world..."
(Mary Oliver)

Frightened of your instability,
ongoing neglect, your carousel of men
pulling me to welcoming laps,
unwelcome touches and more,
I fled as far and fast as I could.

You called. You begged. You sobbed.
I'm better now. I love you. I need you.
How could you leave me? You cursed.
Eavesdropping on the terrifying world
inside of you, of me, I took a hike.

To magic mountains, eons away,
I ran from you. Tried to drink
from the cup of oblivion to negate
despair. Your shadow follows me.
It tears down everything I build.

Alone, but bound to you.
Can I exist without you, mother?
You chew me up and spit me out.
Haunted by your ever-hungry wraith
my hunger for your love, pulls on me.

If I sacrifice myself to you, will it be enough?
If I leave you, will you survive without me?
Wrong question, your shadow whispers.
Without you will I be all right? Will my
soul wither and die? No more, I say!

I lock your memory air-tight and pray.
I throw you in the ocean, far away.
I disremember your name in need.
I forge other links, my own child.
You persist on clouding my sleep.

For my child, my children now, I must
survive. I search for miles until a mirror
shows my true face, my desire. With tears,
I say good-by. To us. To my wish for us.
Finally, free! I fly back to the world

2020 Vision

Jack Cassada

20/20 vision
Means I use both eyes
20/20 vision
Means I see both sides

Balancing open mindedness
With critical thinking skills
Pursuing my own interests;
Leaving room for other wills

Will 2020 bring us clarity
On what's right and wrong
With you and me?

Get us organized
Not polarized?

Will we just keep fighting
Amongst ourselves
While the world around us
Goes straight to hell?

Have you got my back
Or will you stab me in it?
Will I be at your service
Or at your throat?

Will we get up, stand up,
Or stand aside and look?
Will we rise above
Or sink into extinction?

Will 20/20 hindsight
Give us insight into the future?

Will we see the way to heal our
Broken dreams,
Broken minds,
Broken hearts, and
Broken homes?

Are we ascending
Into higher dimensions
Or is that a euphemism
For annihilation?

Is our planet
The Titanic
And all we have left
Is time for one last waltz
As we sink into the abyss,
Shattering to asteroids
In nuclear oblivion
With masses of plastic bags
Floating like swarms
Of jellyfish through space?

Following the Internal Compass

Crickyt J.
Expression

Compassion—
the simple act
of using one's heart
as a compass,

navigating interactions
with environments
encountered while
caring about more
than oneself

Counted

Joan Casey

the refrigerated trucks shown on TV
to carry the dead to where   I wondered
if the numbers would be greater than other wars.

Each day, each hour the counts are taken
of the stricken, the dead while we wonder
if they would be greater with more tests read.

There are counts of masks needed
and first responders lost without them
and counts of beds prepared but not used.

Numbers of the unemployed climb the chart
of a mountain that grows steeper
and we wonder what we are winning or losing.

When I had counted thirty-four days
to letting the idea of Covid 19 be real,
I could not write a word   until the day

I walked and from a distance talked
to the gentle man who cares for his demented wife and
surprised myself saying "I love you."

I stopped at my door to count the thirteen birds
who sat and sang to each other in my just-leafing tree
and I wrote about what I counted

and what counted –
saying "I love you."

A Mother's Love

Norma Cofresi

I.

Magic rocks and shells,
each, its own story.
An oval brown seed,
treasure unearthed
in a hidden forest.
A crushed pink flower
picked for his mother.
Riches unmeasured
in a boy's pocket.
A thin brown branch
transforms to wand,
a rifle, an insect poker.
Toy wooden trains
derail on blue tracks.
Tiny, tin cars crash
call for assistance.
Small red-clad rescuers
arrive at the scene.
Small hands fill buckets
at the river's edge.
Eyes crinkle with laughter
when his sister shrieks.
Little feet outrun waves
under watchful eyes.
Sleepy ride home,
her loving arms enfold,
his breathing unhindered.

II.

A knock on the door
an out of breath neighbor,
a face open in shock.
Words barely heard
regret to inform of a
son's senseless death.
A mother's loss, unabated,
despite medals or protests.
Forever a space where life
used to be. Tumble-down
waves, icy and wrenching.
A son breathes no more.
His last word is Mom.
A cry for her help.
His soul reaches out
her presence a beacon.
In death he remembers
his heart beat with hers.

A Bridge Named Brotherhood

Jack Underhill

> *"There was a bridge named Brotherhood*
> *Made of steps, prophecy and fire.*
> *I did not know that my face*
> *Was a ship that sails inside a spark."*--Adonis

What is Brotherhood?
The Prophet said we should
Love our neighbor as ourselves,
Even the Samaritan, our enemy.

At the Olympics, there is
Brief Brotherhood and Sisterhood
Of toil, sweat, tears, and glory.

In the Great War there was
A short-term Brotherhood of Allies:
The Communists and Capitalists
Against the Fascists.
Then came the cold war: we were no longer Brothers.

There is the Brotherhood of
Religion where we share a set of beliefs
At home and on a foreign shore.
But then we kill those of lesser Gods

There is the dangerous Brotherhood and Sisterhood
Of love that crosses all boundaries of class, religion, and race.

There is the Brotherhood of the Earth
Where all men and fellow creatures
Share the same life-giving air and water.

I am your Brother.
Even for a brief time.

A Friendship Sonnet

Linda Partee

It's not about a cruise, the sporty car
or big bucks in the bank that slip away;
it's friendships we have made both near and far
which warm our hearts with thoughts of yesterday.

Companions sent to us by providence,
perhaps for brief encounters – sometimes long,
who grant our composition evidence
that life's unique concerto plays their song.

So, treasured friends of olde and dear old friends,
now realize the notes you've played for us,
those memorable sounds each instrument lends
to life's ensemble, care and happiness.

Rejoice!   Remember!   Listen once again...
each rich sonata plays on without end.

Nature's View
of
the Grand Design

What Passes and What Merely Stands

J. Scott Wilson

I watch ocean waves roll in
Generated by randomness
Or forces so wild as the wind
Which can only create things askew
And the waves roll in
As you know
In lines
After lines
Upon lines

And we construct
First with our pens and our rulers
Then our hammers
And concrete and steel
We make lines
And lines
Connecting lines

But despite our obsessive engineering
To strive for the sharpest angle
And strive for the lines to define and then defeat forces
It is the randomness of those waves
That will be the perfectors of lines
Marching lines
After lines
Falls after climbs

Do you doubt their perfection?
That is haughty, egotistical like the party line
And it is in vain
For one day your lines will fall apart
But the waves, in lines, will roll in still
Unengineered and falling apart all day

Still they come in lines

Prophetic Pandemics

Dawn Riddle

Pandemics increase
spread lies and disease
affect all we perceive

Nature flares and ruins
integrity of nations
clashes cultures
sears populations.

Human ego deceives, for
intolerant plagues are
more than black and white,
viral cults of personality
breeding grounds for hypocrisy.

Abraham Accord
Fights Mid East discord
Entreats a false peace.

Ancient scrolls have foretold
fallen earth's death throes
dangers of Biblical proportion
climatic scenes of wrong vs. right. . .

Holy scriptures prophetically expose
underpinnings of hastening catastrophes,
divine reckoning for willful state of souls,
Reveal eventual supernatural restoration
Godly peace on a heavenly New Earth.

Mindful

Serena Fusek

On the pond's bank
sit still
as the egret. Let gnats
and mosquitoes swarm
until they grow bored. Let
your eyes become water
through which light passes
easily as fish.

Let the trees--
bark and leaf
climb of ivy
tangle of honeysuckle
slide through your vision.
See the yellow flower,
spy the tiny orchid nestled
among the leaf mold.

Then the hawk materializes
on the branch. You find the deer child
hidden in the thicket. The raccoon
slips to water
washes its clever paws
as you watch and
the small brown sparrows
flitting through last year's brown leaves
lose their invisibility.

You see
the eyes   leaf green
hawk gold   soft as the doe's
watching you.

Israel Revealed

Rabbi Israel Zoberman

Once again to behold you
Long-awaited, longed-for shores.
To awaken and find you
Etched on my horizon line.
Never mind a sleepless night
Hours lost to gain you,
Knowing that my melody
Hums reborn within you.

Fixing It

Vanessa Jones

Everything in this world
absolutely everything
can be fixed with a hammer
and some tape
and maybe a screwdriver
if it's especially broken.

My son points to a bottle of lotion
with a split cap and says "tape!"
and hurries downstairs to bring it back.
We sit on his Mother Goose rug
taping caps, and books, and boo-boos
on teddy bears.

All summer we tape books
and cabinets
and art projects
plastic shovels and golf clubs.
We hammer floors and dressers
and tables and the occasional doll
or baseball.

Then fall finds us,
and we watch the leaves fly
away from the trees, fluttering
on their backs like beetles
dying.

This time of year saddens me
the way it breaks our perfect
summer routine. There will be
less playing outdoors now.
Less picnics, and silly summer songs on the swing.
And in the spring I will have a different boy
and this summer of easy fixes
will never come again.

The leaves pile up, the sandbox grows cold.
The sun dims far before bed.
I pick up a red leaf and point
to the huge tree where it belongs.
"Tree broken," my son says
and he runs inside
for the hammer, and the tape,
and the screwdriver, just in case.
When he returns, we match the leaves
to their trees,
smoothing and taping
A jeweled mosaic to each trunk,
and for good measure he hits each one
with the hammer, like he's hanging paintings.

When it's time for lunch,
we cross the lawn and look back
at what we've done.
The cold trees seem warmer now,
with the leaves coming up their trunks
like mismatched knee socks.
And momentarily it seems we've fixed
a broken season.

Or else my sense of loss at time passing
has been stopped by the boy with the hammer
whose skin will always smell of summer.
I can no longer see the trees for the leaves,
but if I could I might see
what will be in another season
far from now
when my son towers over me.

Espejitos

Carolyn Kreiter-
Foronda

Glasswing butterflies, luminous as crystal,
    stretch your wings in a wind flurry.
        Soar toward asters, oleanders
poisonous as nightshade. Like a predator,
    feed on turgid petals,
        magenta and saffron,
until your gossamer wings become deadly.
    Ward off vultures, hawks, caracaras.
        Thwart evil with your magnetic charm.
Bewitch reserves and parks from Guanacaste
    to Monteverde. With your little mirrors,
        enchant the rainforest
as you dance among patches of bluebells
    and forget-me-nots.
        Who can forget you
disappearing, carrying forty times
    your own weight, your see-through
        wings: thin veils
of reflective glass? Come closer, *espejitos*.
    Cast warmongers, dictators, oppressors
        under your spell,
your stained-glass appearance on sunflowers:
    a celestial sign. With your charisma
        cross borders. Encircle the world.
Stave off pollution, violence, the corruption
    of young minds. Who will ignore
        your divine purpose then?

Covenant Dawn

Janice Hoffman

When the demon of despair
descends and crashes arrogantly
through the secret chambers
of my soul, I remember
the echo of that ancient voice:
"I have set before you
life and death. Choose life."

When the valley of the shadow
of death taunts, torments,
and threatens, I remember
that shards and broken pieces
can be put back together
to create a mosaic of hope like light
through stained glass windows.

Some people may call it
avoidance, but I call it survival
and embrace the holy words
of that old apostle: "If there be
any virtue, anything lovely
and just, anything praiseworthy—
think on these things."

I lie on my bed and *do* think.
I remember that most clichés
are truth, that tomorrow always
follows the heaviest night,
that first light always arrives,
that daybreak comes softly
each morning, again and again.

Norma Cofresi   # El Rodadero
(Rolling Mountain), Yauco, Puerto Rico

My mother's people
know the Tao of the land:
when to plant and when to harvest,
where to dig for fiber-rich
yucca, yautía, yams, and ñame:
tubers with thick brown skins
peeled, boiled, drizzled with
olive oil or rendered fatback
from slaughtered pigs.

My mother's people
are one with the land.
They hold reverence
for the sacred and ineffable,
pray to Papá Dios
y a Madre Santa
to heal and restore,
and to help each one
follow the good path.

My mother's people
are mountain dwellers.
Each new day welcomed,
each birth a celebration.
Each death a heart-piercing good-by.
Hurricanes, droughts,
 and floods are seasonal afflictions,
but tremor after tremor,
bewilder even the wise.
For weeks unrelenting

71

earthquakes shift the earth.
The ground trembles the land
awake, rests, moves again.
Pink, yellow, and bright blue
houses tumble down hills,
 onto driveways, blocking roads.
 In the wide spaces, away from trees
 and houses, my people sleep.

An old Lady keeps watch
with her lit cigar.
She is one with
the goddess of the land.
She grieves with the land,
tears of anguish from her eyes fall.
She grieves inconsolably, she weeps.
She stomps her foot in anger
and in her wake brings forth renewal.

Consider Needs Carefully

Linda Partee

Put down light footprints on our earth
beside the ancients' fur-bound feet;
let sight and deeds renew world's worth,
whose fading image can't compete

with riches found below its crust
and dwindling forests yet to fell.
Man's progress drives a selfish lust
to curb before life's final knell.

Restore our soil for growing food,
and water safe for fish and drink;
each voice and picture must intrude
right now, to save man from the brink.

Imagine yesteryear's clear skies,
unspoiled lagoons, lakes, rivers, streams;
you know it's time to do what's wise--
return to man these precious dreams.

Airborne Epidemic Invisible Thing

J. Scott Wilson

It's like this classic horror movie *The Thing*
something's right on the other side of the door
and you don't know what to do about it before it busts through
     and destroys you,
       en masse

So much is irrelevant,
     There are odds based on age
     strength
     other immune factors
Compromises are one of the only social factors
     you seem to understand
The other is society itself
While I need
     we need
     all the humans need to be
together
     you need
     you need us
     you need all humans to be
together

Society can be our friend
     even while friends may stab us in the back
But eversomore
     than whispers behind a door
     I have to protect against you chilling my core
     and suit up just to head to the store

But because of you we're supposed to disband
      and non-compliers reprimand
But because of factors of age
      strength
      lack of immune detractors
I am the one perched between three worlds
I am the safe set of lungs to shield those who need "the more"
      but dare not risk the grocery store

Yet what I have that they do not
is but a thin veil
      my immunity may not prevail
Even now, walking the aisles stocking my grandmother's house
      I am no less vulnerable than a mouse
I feel you sting my eyes, dot my skin,
                  questing within,
      while I try to complete my task
I swear I can smell you even through this surgical mask
      While I try to keep my composure
      not succumb to you, sir.
While tendrils prick my arms travelling
      the long, dark hallway that is quarantine

Airborne illness like this classic horror movie
      The Invisible Man
He could be right here reaching out with his hand
At your throat
      imperative to breathe, gripped, can't understand
      but you'll destroy me
(and mine)   *en masse*

I See Beyond The Stars

G. Barry

I see beyond the stars
Where others cannot be
And feel the ocean waves
Below a moonlit sea
The deepest darkest depths
An unmeasured restless soul
Abound forever in me
With all I do not know
Forever will I ponder
'Til death will I always fear
That I will ne'er be able
To see my thoughts revealed

When Dawn Spills

Ann Shalaski

I planted a flower
in an open field
not far from the house,

except instead of a flower,
it became a tree.
And the house became a clock,

tilted slightly to the right.
Still, I was happy.
This was a good sign,

more than I had hoped for.
There are some who say,
I just don't understand.

But I see beauty in the tree,
faces of relatives,
and even my own.

And when dawn spills
over the roof every day
at 6 am,

I'm struck by the morning glories
I never noticed before,
giving thanks.

A Figment of Our Imagination Tastefully Done

Barbara Drucker
Smith

We heard it on the grapevine
To be fruitful and multiply
That's the berries
And berry, berry good
So start with a date
With your favorite peach

According to the greens organization
You can beat the energy crisis by going
Greens and preserving the earth
Oranging for world cooperation
By squashing and mediating disagreements

Bean there and stewed
So snap out of it
By working with pears
To keep more people olive

By working for peas and hominy
For ourselves and our nations
And for all people
And always avocadoration for God

Through Borrowed Eyes

What Blazes the Trail is Not Necessarily Pretty

Joan Casey

*A poem written with my grand-
daughter, Zoe Floyd's, words*

Zoe was sixteen when she joined EMS. She thinks Rescue Squad runs
in her blood.
Considering her parents met "running squad," and
both grandmothers and a slew of aunts and uncles trained in the
medical profession
she's probably right.
For Zoe, the volunteer rescue squad is family:
"You don't dedicate at least twelve hours of your day
on the front lines and not develop a strong bond
with the people you share your worst and best experiences."

Now that Zoe is eighteen and in charge of her own unit,
she can look back and say "I think I expected what everyone
expects,
what you see on TV – medics taking care of very sick people.
In reality, most calls I run are not hectic, running around trying to
save someone's life.
Sometimes I simply help someone up and take their dog out for
them.
But don't get me wrong.
There is the controlled chaos of a cardiac arrest ...
a profuse bleed-out of a patient's nose who is hooked up to a
ventilator."
These all are what Zoe calls "good calls" –
"ones that I walk away from knowing I made a difference and
helped someone."

What Zoe didn't expect in running rescue was to cry for eighteen
hours straight
after she responded to a mother's call about her daughter.
Zoe recalled what the room looked like.
"The walls were painted blue.
The closet was on the right wall behind the door.
Her bed was to the left of the door.
There was a tall lamp by the closet.
I turned the lights on in her room."

What blazes the trail is not necessarily pretty.

"She was lying on her back, almost propped up on her pillows.
She had a stuffed animal in her arms
and her phone lying to the right of her charging.
Her charger had one of those cute animal accessories
to protect it from breaking.
She was ashen gray.
There was vomit staining her mouth and chest and blankets."

"She was fifteen and had committed suicide.
I connected that with my suicide attempt at fourteen
and her age was between the ages of my two sisters."
For Zoe, this was a "bad call."
When TOD (time of death) was announced,
she walked downstairs to get some air and recuperate
and overheard a police officer tell the mother,
"You need to stay down here right now.
The EMT's and paramedics are doing their best to try and save your
daughter."

Back inside the ambulance for privacy, Zoe burst into tears.
For her, it was "gut wrenching knowing
that at the same moment the officer was telling the mother we were
saving her life,
we had just declared her dead."

Zoe's first collected thought was, "this isn't going to make me quit.
From that moment, I knew I was dedicated to EMS."

What blazes the trail is not necessarily pretty.
But Zoe is.
She has soft brown eyes and a mass of curly hair.

Who are the Immigrants?

Sharon Dorsey

We are called Indians,
Native Americans,
First People,
Indigenous Americans.
We answer to all, if spoken with respect.

But don't name your sports teams after us.
Don't teach your children to play games
of cowboys and Indians unless
the Indians are sometimes the good guys too.

Oh, and if you are barring immigrants from this land,
remember, unless you answer to one of those names...
Indians, Native Americans, First People,
Indigenous Americans...YOU are an immigrant here.

We let you in and taught you to survive in the wilderness.
You repaid us by stealing our lands,
and murdering sixty-three-million of us.
What gives you the right to decide who stays and who goes?

Instead, it's time to pay it forward...
to allow struggling and threatened families in,
to share in the bounty of the land of the free
and the home of the brave,

as we allowed you in,
and shared with you.

Ceramic Secrets

Crickyt J. Expression

With fine pristine white crack
running along its swell,
a small blue vase
sits high upon the shelf,
'20 inscribed on round clay base.

In *our* collective memory,
with flowers it's never been graced.
No sprigs of dried baby's breath
ever adorned the rim.
Yet, daily,

her trembling feather duster
caresses the ceramic glaze
like a lingering kiss.

When we question the vessel's origin
or how the fracture came to be,
her soft wrinkled face
assumes far away gaze,
birthing mournful pause.

In seasoned wisdom's voice
she says--

It was a gift,
a token from careless years.
The crack bears witness
to a moment when
I should have replied with

'yes.'

George Floyd

Rabbi Israel Zoberman

R.I.P.
Thank you, George Floyd, for making sure
That 2020 will be remembered not only for
An inflicting Coronavirus but even more so
For a revolution of the heart inspired by an
Unassuming gentle spirit in a giant's frame
Who taught us all-white, black and brown -
That a simple man, no celebrity, could hopefully
Change the world his loving spirit charged,
Awakening with divine grace sleepy multitudes,
Whose last breath of agonizing 8 minutes,
46 seconds, we count sacred with Mr. Floyd
Becoming a household name though not born a prince
While you wanted just to breath like fellow
Humans gifted by God's birthright at least another
Day, and heavenly mama would gladly wait,
Destined in death to accomplish
Unwittingly what you could not alive do.
Forgotten you will never be, roaming with
Angels among the stars to protect dear ones left
Behind, but your excruciatingly aching neck stomped
By a bending knee not in homage to the gods,
Is a transforming symbol now for the oppressor's
Universal rod which together we are bent to break apart,
As the dying cry, "Man, I can't breathe,"
Will ever echo from Sea to Shining Sea.

Housing While Black in Clear View

Shanya
  Lady S

Manifest Destiny- man infested destiny
starting in 14th century
killing off Native Men and taking over countries

Gentrification- the process of getting rid of
the last generation of people that lived in the hood
Rename it add new people and call it good.

Re-gentrification - means we liked there before now we want it
back.
Once called "Indian Giving" but it's Euro-driven in fact.

Amenity- a feature in a house you can't afford
if you break it, I'll tape it I'm a good Landlord

Landlord- the person who owns your house always in control,
you pay the bills, they make the rules.
They have rights, we are fools.

Application- a way to deny
any idea that you will ever qualify

Taxes- a way to still take property back from a brother

Clear title- you have it clear and free any questions
refer back to taxes don't pay them
and give it back to "Uncle Sam"

Personal property- stuff that's not even considered real,
proof that you spend money on stuff without knowing the deal

i.e. shoes, jewelry and all things that depreciate

PUD- Planned Unit Development- you pay us to keep you in your place,
we keep you in check so you don't mess up our space

Real estate- the only real wealth

Hood- a tight jacket that keeps all who don't fit elsewhere in one place

H.O.A.- Having Other Avenues to keep you in place

Gated Community- a physical gate to keep you out our space

JP Morgan, Wells Fargo, M&T, Bank of America, Citigroup they see you
make sure that housing while black is in clear view

On Being Non-White

Ed Lull

Can we ignore what isn't right
when it's been wrong four hundred years?
To kill or maim to show our might,
survivors left to drown in tears?

How could forebears not realize
how inhumane it was to see
the evil dance before their eyes
yet take no steps to disagree?

> They understand that they are free,
> but seldom find equality.

The opportunities for whites
in education, jobs, and health
are often called their human rights
that open doors to gaining wealth.

For non-whites things are not the same,
they often hear 'that same old song'
with attitudes that should hold shame
but just imply: "You don't belong."

> They understand that they are free,
> but seldom find equality.

In uniform they fought with pride,
but now a uniform means fear.
Police will pull non-whites aside
as if non-whites pose threats severe.

For many, faith renews their strength,
and hope says wrongs may soon be right.
For love they'll go to any length
in prayer to make their future bright.

> They understand that they are free,
> but seldom find equality.

Spitting Poetry

(For James DeVille)

Ann Shalaski

I used to think you had no message,
until you finally broke free.
The day you spoke clearly about life.

Words dropped from your lips
in elegant verses the color
of heartache and salvation.

I used to think you had no message,
until you spoke of a place to put pain.
The need to reclaim ourselves.

The fullness of a glass. No substance,
I once thought, until I saw you pace
the stage as if circling a flight pattern.

Gather images like kindling that burst
into flames giving light to the things
that haunt you.

I see you, poet, and I am not surprised.
Tenderness was deep inside, the message
was in you.

Just as a soul is in the body, and cream
is in the milk. We are hungry for truth,
waiting like children to be fed.

And this is good. We will be alright.
In fact, we've never been better. Thank you
for the fuel, the fire is in us now.

Stray Dog Signs of Armageddon

J. Scott Wilson

We hold these truths to be self evident
      But for barely more than 200 years

The stray dog that tries to settle in my yard
Showed me signs of declining nation
Lessons learned and rituals saved
Are ghosts of domestication

Habits kept may be survival signs
He still makes nests of newspaper trash to pee
He's trouble here, I chase him away
And he questions why I do so desperately

He wants to know if it's really him
Or is it the habits he's started to shirk
Habits sociability needed tick away
He'll get down to just that which works

Next time I chase him off he postulates
That I'm superstitious of what he represents
Until you have to ask "What is really survival?"
Then there another learned habit went

It felt better to go off on your own
So starting when you gave master the slip
Habits of amity and association started this exodus
Like so many rats leaving a sinking ship

Then dog challenged me
Follow my life metaphor of walking a path
Sometimes more paved
And clearly made
And other times it's rough
And barely enough

Many times you take a fall
And after enough falls you come
      To trust that surely
           Another fall will come

Waiting for the next fall turns one off of trying to even step forward
Walker may have to sit
Sitter may decide cowering is better
Cringing gives way to lying flat

The final societal habit to shirk is trying

Cultivating Flames

Crickyt J. Expression

I light a candle today
as again realities sway
remembering those lost
brings to mind the cost
The flame a reminder
of the lives squandered
when violence overtakes
and ends in heartbreaks

I light a candle today
searching for a shared way
to see through the sadness
understand the madness
The flame reflective
seeking deeper perspective
on lessons to be learned
as history's pages are turned

I light a candle today
envisioning clearly the day
when we seek to be better
and learn to work together
To the hues of the flame
I whisper their names—
the black lives taken,
now, as ancestors awaken

I light a candle today,
protests fill streets each day
decrying racism in all forms
facing lines of blue uniforms
My flame is lit not in sorrow
but hope of a new tomorrow
as children play 'Tag- I Got You!'
at the base of a used to be statue

Lost Souls

Sharon Dorsey

He sits alone in his 12 x 14 room,
isolated from fellow-residents,
abandoned by his family.

Staff brings food three times a day
but he's afraid to eat it because
they are not wearing gloves or masks.

When he tries to advocate for safety,
staff calls his family members
and brands him a "trouble-maker."

His contact with the outside world
is the television's grim statistics or
an occasional call from a friend.

Nobody tells him if the evil virus
has invaded his premises, claimed
friends. Staff says it's a privacy issue.

So he waits, forbidden to walk past other
closed-door rooms to reach the outside,
breathe fresh air, revel in the birth of spring.

He waits and wonders what lies ahead.
He is past his eighty-fifth year – reconciled
to dying – but hoping for more life,
for more springs.

Self Beyond

~

A Step Outside

Renovations

Terra Leigh

He points at me and laughs,
Ridicules my attempts
To follow the pack of people
Walking to their next chapter.

I bury my head in prayers,
But requests go unanswered.

Instead,
God hands me
A hammer
And points to the walls.

As I go from day to day,
No settings change.
My vision blurs.

I start chiseling away
At the beige surroundings
With His verses.

One hole,
And I find traces
Of a new smile.

Another hole,
And I find new poems.

Every morning,
I set aside time
To knock down more walls
In this monotony

Just to find
The treasures God buried here.

Not Seen, but Known

Serena Fusek

The poem is the fox in the underbrush
barely more than a flash of eyes and auburn
and a whiff of its musk on the evening air.

It is the three does
glimpsed in the headlights
on a dark road--
a head raised, ears swiveling
a glimpse of white...
gone..

Action in an alley
caught in the corner of our seeing
like a piece of grit
accretes into a poem.

The poem is not found in the room
but in the mirror. What happens
in the room beyond the mirror's frame--
a glance of skirt swirl
a trousered leg--
can only be guessed: a dance?

In the thick heat
that stuns the afternoon.
poplars, maples
honeysuckle and the privet it's tangled in
exhale chlorophyll and oxygen--
a nimbus of hazy respiration
shimmering through humidity--

science
or just poetry?

Dip the bucket into the well
draw it up
and when the pail reaches the top
sun drops into the water
explodes like glass
across our vision.
On our tongues
the taste of cold and stone

across our eyes
a veil of dazzle.

Of Human Bonding

Linda Partee

Her evil known...daringly heard or seen
covertly from a hidden annex room.
For twenty-five months, their hideout held eight
who wouldn't stand beneath the moon or sun;
go out to exercise, obtain supplies;
forsake their safety due to tedium.

Betrayed by malice, or perhaps by chance,
preparedness still formed a crack or leak
where uniformed enemies barged inside,
abruptly ending long-lived sacrifice,
resolve, endurance, courage, hopes and dreams.
A sole survivor left to carry on.

Our mind-bending evil's unheard, unseen
overtly, other than by microscope.
Humanity, gambled like slot machines,
each hour, each day, no certain end in sight.
It's early witnessing drama unfold,
while many comforts need surrendering.

Betrayed by carelessness or ignorance,
perhaps too slow preparing--loved ones lose.
As masked crusaders war with pestilence,
await supplies, assistance, beg for cures,
insensitive behaviors forge ahead
and virus reaches toward our breaking point.

Consider this an opportunity
to weigh priorities and rearrange;
for dusting cobwebs off our better selves,
professing gratitude for what we have.
Just who will be among survivors now?
It took disease to learn we're bound as One.

Student of the Drive, 1985/2020

J. Scott Wilson

What I can't tell my son, seventeen
       see,
behind the wheel he terrifies me.
But if he knew the secret
that'd be the end,
       off the edge every time the road takes a bend.
I'm afraid this generation is just not as sensory
       as mine and me.

Neil Peart, god rest his soul,
       brought it out whole
Taught my generation how to merge
how to think of one's *self* purged
of the frailties of flesh
with the metals and plastics enmeshed
Like embalmed my blood replaced
oil/antifreeze switching degrees behind the face

But, no for myself I found it first
when pulled along for the ride
clasped to German made steel
but with no motor, all glide

The rise of the thrill
wasn't just early morning chill
it was well engineered will
clanking up the lift hill

Loch Ness Monster, morning mists
forgiving the Walkman of the tape's hiss

Opening strains of "One Vision" by Queen
completed me, coaster and music
      a three part machine.
Fusion to the thing completed
      as the wheels roll free
and the first blast of guitar
      signals the end of a separate me.
Thrown to the ground
      back up by the fifth guitar sound.
Engineered to feel dangerous on the experience's face
      engineered safe at the same pace
Less than 2 minute ride
      yet born, lived and died
and reincarnated into the same familiar, mundane place.

And that's how I learned to drive a car, too.
      Something that every damn state trooper knew
a Ferrari lives in my blue Toyota grocery-getter,
      but "Son, you oughtta know better"
and they're still stroking out the ticket to me.

But they weren't cursing my hide
      when they cranked the cruiser up to one-thirty-five.
No, they weren't just driving a car
they didn't have to peel-out too far
to emerge as a shooting star
      a target tracking warship
      that I could never give-the-slip
You know they feel it, too,
      this sensation of becoming something outside of you
Thankful for the chance to rattle the manifold
Wind through the grille, set the jawline steely-cold.

No,   more alive they've never felt
than when sinews stretch into serpentine belts.

Three generations of men and women were bred
        with mechanical notions alive in their heads.
From Springsteen's suicide machines littering Highway Nine
        'til waiting to drive again feels like doing time
I realized that this might be a thing
        over which we used to sing,
            that the two recentest generations
            might not get as 'a thing.'
And if I taught my son to fill his senses with the car
        that might drive his distraction too far.
Where becoming one with the machine was the point in 1985
        I need him to climb out of the metal alive
So I focus on that as the mission
        and god forbid I try to teach him on manual transmission.

This I Use

G. Barry

I have turned it off
Turned twenty-twenty off
I've walked away
I don't want to see
What twenty-twenty
Has placed before me

Searching for sanctuary
I wonder and wander
Tears welled up
As meaning is lost
And words – words

Seeking refuge
Where it cannot find me
A hideout
From it all
One with Mother Earth

I lay my body
Down in a steam
A catafalque I am not worthy of
To change the water's course
I know not everlasting
But – in this moment
Alter its ebb and flow

Its current is destined
To a place I cannot go
Far away from my altered dream

I see its change ends
Where the ripples
Cascade over my toes

If I lie here for an eternity
Could its course perhaps change
Could I redirect the valleys
And cause my wanton change
Or – would she alter me

How do I write
The words inside of me
Through the filters
Of my mind
So twenty-twenty
Is safe and clear
And I can let
The darkness go
And truly see

Stream of Consciousness

Lorraine Benedetto

It was strangely framed, a bit obtuse
as 'seedlings' go...the opening line
    This I use to alter the world was clear
as a bell – but what was one to make of
    so I can see it in 2020?
Change the world so I can see the world?

And yet
there was something satisfyingly jarring
about the phrasing. Something *so* American-ly
disjointed about it.
Like seeing homeless people sleeping
in the doorways of Tiffany's and Versace,
or hearing protesters chant
"Keep your Government paws
out of my Medicare".

It *shake-rattle-&-roll* ed
in my skull for months
      drumming away
at my subconscious.

In the end,
I took refuge
in literal...

Sidestepping
the Alice-in-Wonderlandish
    vortex
  threatening to blur
my beleaguered 20-20
      vision.

Mere Magic

Terra Leigh

With a flick of her wrist,

Fires morph
Into sunny days.

Failures rip off their masks
To become second chances.

Deaths and lost ships
Reopen bridges for new people.

Another day tucked at home
Is another day God lays foundations
Without us stepping into his wet cement.

And the history
Of stifling news reports
And exploding arguments online
Become echoes of the subconscious.

Then, she sets down
Her pencil
And takes her first breath.

She's ready for what will come next.

Whimsical

Anne Emerson

My poems aren't satirical,
nor are they political.
Most often they are lyrical;
I've written one not typical.
For me, it is a miracle.

More Visible by Guess

Serena Fusek

In the mirror's flat sheen
my face floats
eyes peering
into eyes.

In the thin glass
the room behind
is duplicated

a still photo

until something
like a ripple
shivers across the surface
and down my spine.

Something hides
deep in the mirror
where the little fishes
glint like stray pieces of moon
something lurks
down in the mud
where the lilies root

something ancient
before earth dreamed
the softness of mammals
something that oozes
its huge bulk--

something more visible
by guess
than glance--

through the murk.

Eddies of its passing
flicker inside the glass

surge through my veins.

In the mirror's flat sheen
my face floats
pale as the moon.

Views Down the Line

~

A Future, The Pasts

Found in the Year the Christmas Cactus Bloomed Four Times

Joan Casey

Blue skies clear of cloud and planes,
roads with few cars in spite of cheaper gas,
along empty tracks, parked trains, and
on my porch, empty pots for planting.

Early one morn, I went back to the eighteenth century
captured in recreated houses and shops,
where only ghosts came out of quarantine
to walk the empty streets with me.

I have gone the mile down Duke of Gloucester
many times as a student, educator, researcher
but never have I seen no one – not one tourist,
not one employee, not one resident – no one.

Memory led me back to where I never really was
learning about life in a time that was not mine,
wondering now if there was a way
to discover yesterday for tomorrow.

Was there really something to find, here
in a garden of century-old herb specimens? or
under the leaves of a four-hundred year-old oak tree
whose limbs touched the ground around me?

I passed the jail that held no prisoners
and the courthouse that was locked up,
on my way to meet my daughter
and granddaughter by the sheep.

The lamb that looked like her favorite stuffed animal,
must have missed the affection of visitors.
It stopped nursing on its mother's full teat
and laid in the grass by the fence for us to pet it.

Down the road, the horses hung their heads
over the fence, eagerly awaiting our arrival
to lick each of our hands,
one by one, and my face.

We turned to leave and saw a field of buttercups waving
in the wind, and I saw what also bloomed
under shutdown-school rules. My daughter and granddaughter
walking away, chatting like two best friends.

I left with bread my daughter made from scratch –
a skill she acquired to meet Covid scarcity.
She also gave me packages of seeds
to plant in the pots on my porch.

In the year the Christmas Cactus bloomed four times,
I found new joy in being alone,
I found the time to look my soul in the face,
and found what was good about yesterday and today
for tomorrow.

Synonyms

Doris Gwaltney

Some people say the words are all the same.
But are they?
Some people say they mean the same.
But do they?
You can fix it
You can change it
Break it or remake it
But you have to do it differently
Now don't you?
So let's grab a book from off the shelf
A heavy dictionary.
For certain people, like certain words
They like to know all letters that bunch up together
They must learn to spell them
They must learn to speak them
And you must understand
Words are the same
And yet they are different

Am I right?
Or am I wrong?

> *From the first moment I saw the digits 2020,*
> *I was fascinated by these numbers. However,*
> *I have met with many troubling problems connected*
> *with 2020. Still, the numbers are able to hold*
> *their place in the world. They are alive. They*
> *refuse to be buried beneath the detritus of the past.*

Not My First Rodeo

Janice Hoffman

Neighbor Kathy had polio and wore braces,
so we used her crutches for rifles.
After all, the 1950s were all
about Westerns, so we obliged.
Classmate Keila couldn't play because
the Health Department put a sign
on their front door saying her dad
was quarantined with TB.

Aunt Irene was secluded before
she died of cancer, so I didn't
get to say good-bye, but Mama
cut down one of her dresses for me,
a red and white gingham check
that fell all the way to the floor.
I put my hair in a bun like a saloon
girl, so I could be Miss Kitty.

We wore cowboy and cowgirl suits—
mine, aqua and my brother's, black—
both with fringes dangling from the sleeves.
We wrestled and wrangled our dog
and called him our dogie, then lassoed
each other with jump rope. When we
played The Lone Ranger, I was Tonto
because I already had long braids.

Measles, chickenpox, and mumps
ran their courses as we stayed inside
or played in the backyard shooting

enemies like Black Bart and diseases.
So, you see, I am not new
to epidemics, pandemics, and isolation.
My entire childhood prepared me.

The Beginning 1926

Barbara Drucker
Smith

Waiting for a street car
A stranger carrying a violin
Bemoans the fact that
He needs an accompanist
A woman offers to be
His piano accompanist
And did so for
The next forty years
The man and woman
Who met by coincidence
Are my mother and father
Music bound them together
Years of attending the
Tanglewood Music Festival
Years of going to local
Community concerts
Years of making music together

I've Heard this Music Before

Peggy Newcomb

I've heard this music before
And danced and made merry.
Listen! Can you hear it now
or does it live in a special memory
burried in the past?

When joints didn't ache with every step
when we were asked if
we'd taken lessons...
You would twirl me about
and end with a death defying dip.
Just to show off.

Oh what fun we had!
I could not keep a straight face
while watching your antics
that you called dancing!

And to think they had the nerve
to ask if we'd had lessons!
Oh yes, I've heard this music before
and you were there!

2020 Vs. 20/20

Rabbi Israel Zoberman

2020 will be known
As the Coronavirus year
When the world we knew
Was so suddenly transformed,
No longer steady to our stumbling feet,
And our 20/20 assuredly
Became beclouded with biting anxiety,
The Rabbis taught that the Corona
Counting the most is the crown
Of a good name,
Virus gives way to virtue,
Violence to vision,
Confrontation to conversation,
Duel to dialogue,
Finally finding the magnificent
In the mundane.

Clear

Serena Fusek

How clearly do I need to see?
Clearly enough to
find the rabbit
in the underbrush
so I can eat.
Clearly enough to realize
the horse has a stone
in its hoof.
To realize the engine
needs work before
it becomes scrap. To see
the child has a fever,
the dog a tick
the biscuits are burning.

Clearly enough to see
when to duck.

Altered Views in 2020

Kathleen Decker

Time alters views...
as a teen
I vowed not to see 2000
as I would be too old and decrepit
in 2020, I view life as precious
and myself as young
true, there are twinges
and morning stiffness
I don't dare fall off a horse
arthritis has already cost me
knitting
and limits beloved violin-playing
but I'm not old, oh no, not me

as a teen
the overwhelming angst
would I achieve my dreams?
in 2020, I have achieved both
more and less, and attained pinnacles
I had no intention of climbing
I count successes
in spite of certain failures
that linger in bad dreams
like molded cheese in that
forgotten corner of the fridge
in bright daylight the view is positive

as a teen
there was pain,
trauma, and loss

that no faith would heal
and so, I lost faith
in 2020, I look back
and nurture myself
listen to my husband
"get over it! That was then, this is now!"
I see so many others
with similar losses and trauma
the teen was anything but alone
and faith has returned

2020 retrospective (re)vision
leaves me wondering
about 2040

Lest We Forget...

Sharon Dorsey

Yes, we live in a racist society.
Yes, brutality is rampant in
our law enforcement culture.
Yes, we have been guilty of apathy.

Black and brown lives do matter.
Fair practices in jobs, housing, matter.
Equal educational opportunities matter.
Access to health care matters too.

But let's not forget, violent oppression of
indigenous people was happening in our
country in the 1400s, long before Africans
were kidnapped and enslaved.

Sixty-three million Native Americans
were slaughtered to make way for white
civilization. Between two and four thousand
Cherokee ancestors died on the Trail of Tears.

Treaties were made and broken, all in the
name of white supremacy and occupation.
History books praised the pioneers for stealing
land and assassinating the original owners.

Protestors now swarm our streets,
crying out for liberty and justice for **all**.
We've heard this music of inequity before
with minimal long-lasting changes.

Why does this time feel different?
Perhaps we've seen too much, for too long...
immigrant children in cages...peaceful protestors
gassed, clubbed...racist murders by police;

too many wrongs; too much blatant brutality
heaped on innocents; or perhaps it's because
a new generation has claimed the streets, beating
the drum for a fair future, vowing, this time, to win.

What I Did

These Hands are My Hands

Timothy Wright

They are old and worn, but they are mine
They have been with me through thick and thin
They have loved and they have killed,
But these are my hands
They have raised three children and survived three wives (so far)
They have held more shot glasses,
                    smoked more cigars,
                                    shaken more hands

They have hugged more people
These hands are blessed
They are currently stained with blue hair dye, fuck it

Penalty of Pleasure

Raymond M.
Simmons

Inside new fantasies You found
New hope comes forth solid and sound.
Knowing where priorities lie,
It becomes clear what you must try.

Inside the borders of the norm.
So many treasures have been stormed.
Reaching ultimate highs in turn
Add to all lessons You have learned.

With sanity in charge of you
Those useless worries fade from view.
To embrace goals you need to reach.
Set standard rules, you must not breach.

Don't let your values take a fall,
Because you seek to have it all.
New skills for new things to do
Will unveil complicated clues.

You see just what you need to see
In the throes of intensity.
You bend and shape your newfound plan
That's right for all to understand.

When unnatural thrills take your breath,
You seek to form a bond with death.
With anxiety you did yearn
To welcome joy when it returns.

The balance of your common sense
Makes joy and laughter more intense
The logic sets inside your brain,
Where pleasant spirits feel no pain.

Ann Shalaski

Opt Out

I'm tempted to wander off, slip out the backdoor,
dissolve into the night. It won't make me new
or strong. But sometimes, disappearing is the only way
to survive. It's a feeling that vibrates inside
like piano strings, churn of a train's wheels leaving
the station. Reminds me of the first time I held
a bird, small heart fluttered in my hand as it struggled
to lift, fly away. I'll leave everything behind.
Clatter of fans, blue jay bickering in the maple.
House flapping like loose skin, fine silk thread
unraveled. Take the folding chair, plaid wool blanket
from the closet. I'll sit, watch leaves filter through branches
clearing their minds. Wait until spring before I return
when impatiens flavor the air with sweetness,
and I've extracted beauty from sorrow. It won't matter
what you tell people. Tell them anything.
That I lost my place, sense of time.
That words withered in my mouth like dried figs.
Tell them absence is a choice.

The 4 Agreements/
The Massacre of Marriage

Shanya
Lady S

1. Be impeccable with your word.
I made a board of visions
He removed all traces of himself
I made a path of provisions
He proclaimed 2 kids and I as wealth
Success, if a picture is worth 1000 words
Then the universe heard my cry

2. Don't take anything personally.
In the end I said it's not me it's you
Removed reasons for sadness from my shoulders
You never wanted children I'll take them too
Removed bills and responsibility like boulders
Stalemate? success? like yogurt
Why let milk sour before adding fruit

3. Don't make assumptions.
"The 5 Love Languages", I read
He read the "Art of War"
I catered to possibilities, now dead
Once he swore, now my soul tore
Failure, I assumed all communication
was part of building a relationship

4. Always do your best.
When my choices are fly or die, I fly
The goal is not knowing where to land

It's reaching for the sky,
Not being stepped on by man
Success, every butterfly was once a caterpillar
Be careful if you catch me crawling, I transform

My Place

Julia Travers

I carry broad round stones
through a curtain of willow braids
and lay them down in a row
in the moss.

They lead to a small clearing
sketched by feathered arms of cedar,
where a big, overstuffed chair waits,
full of fresh white pillows
and soft gray blankets,
its legs rooted to the earth,
its back and arms cradled by a
family of sleepy boulders
laden with pale lichen.

Here,
I smell honeysuckle
and rich, dark soil.
The ocean, just down the lane,
breathes deep
in my ear.

I sit with my legs curled up beside me.
My wild hair is pinned back with branches.
Birds land nearby and eat the sunflower seeds
I scatter from my lap.
I trace the spiral of a new fern.
Sun and shadow paint my quiet face.

Here,
I'm not worried about you.
My love comes your way
of its own accord.

Enough is Enough

Anne Emerson

We think the small aggressions
cannot be worth the fight.
That's true, if what we try
are normal ways to fight.
But here's what I've been told
by the "lowest of the low."

Do not hit back, but neither
co-operator be.
Leave the room.
Walk away.
Divorce the one you love.
Tell mother she's not welcome
at your house anymore.
Never, never, never
engage.

This, Gandhi recognized,
and roused his countrymen.
Together they moved mountains,
but rot grew rank within.
The enemy defeated –
they turned upon their own.

It's time for us, as well,
to tell it like it is:
"The garbage – we can see it,
and it is not OK."

So, have you heard the voices
of victims of abuse?
Do not hit back, but neither
co-operator be.
Leave the room.
Walk away.
Divorce the one you love.
Tell mother she's not welcome
at your house anymore.

And how might we, so small,
outside the halls of power,
rebuke them – "Cut it out"?
We will not buy their goods,
but work with friends we know.
And dress ourselves in homespun,
or break some laws in peace
to cook a little salt.

And would we kill our leader
with all our battles won?
Let's keep the rot away
from our insides and our own.

Within ranks, as without:
do not hit back, but neither
co-operator be.
Leave the room.
Walk away.
Divorce the one you love.
Tell mother she's not welcome
at your house anymore.

Never, never, never
Engage.

Unnatural, you ask?
No, think again, I say.
It's normal not to fight –
to want to walk away.

But here we are, today,
with no place else to go.
And when this fight is won –
I hope it will be won –
it's God who gets to choose
the saints who live or die.

Can we lay down our arms –
and that includes our lies –
the ways we tell ourselves,
"I'll do what's good for me;
no harm can come of it"?

I've had to tell my heart –
which weak and human cries –
that, if it will offend me,
then yes, I know to break it.
And, if my foot offends me,
then I will cut it off.
And likewise, sinful eyes.
I'll take myself in hand
and teach me to behave.
I'll watch the spitting child
within me throw a fit.
I'll laugh at it – it's funny –

and it will creep away.

And no, I'm not to blame
if others won't behave.
It may be, I will choose
to stand my ground in silence
and watch a lost-one kill me.

Is that what I believe in?
So, will I let her kill me?
Although I have no weapon,
might I still redeem her?

Help! I'm Going MAD!

Peggy Newcomb

Write a poem
my good friend suggest
but if you're bored
you have nothing to say.

Thank God for Ken Burns,
The National Parks,
Space Exploration, two million
year old dinosaur bones discovered in
Australia And how scientist proved
there is a hole in the stratosphere.

Oh how educated I've become
these days...I've even taken notes
on making a few Greek dishes!
Nothing's out of my reach!
Stand back!
Who knows what's next. You may have
to be polite and taste my latest creation...
that'll be tricky with social isolation!

Well now you know
I'm going MAD!
I've even had my computer
repaired!!

Altered by 2020

Crickyt J.
Expression

Messages are saved,
the mundane and profound;
they could be final

Friend's pages scanned
for signs of life;
death is a thief

Goodbye is hated,
hanging heavy in the air,
a looming threat

'Be Safe' as farewell
serves adults like
childhood nightlights;

it won't stop monsters
or grabbing shadows,
and won't hold the Reaper at bay,
it just helps us sleep.

Lifelines

Lorraine Benedetto

THIS I use
to alter the world
so I can see
      [hope]
in twenty-twenty.

THIS tapestry line
of like minded peeps
snaking through
              streets
protesting abuse.

THIS multi-ply mask
of close woven threads
sculpted to press
tight to my
      cheeks
in mindful defense.

THIS cellulose sheaf
printed en masse
(black lines on white field)
presenting the
chance

to nudge destiny's
path.

A Pandemic Offering

S.A. Borders-
Shoemaker

Do we see the body
as a conduit for the soul
the thing that conjures
the fire of our anger
joy, and passion?

Do we understand
the written word
as the ultimate communication
of humankind in their
imperfect capacity?

Without inhibition
these forces collide
and it is poetry
I use to transform
my reality into
healing clarity.

Careful consideration
mingled with
precise beauty-
this is what I bring
to 2020.

A Very Scary Fairy Tale

Sharon Dorsey

Once upon a time, there was a beautiful land
suddenly attacked by a silent, invisible enemy.
Thousands of citizens perished.

The people could no longer go to work or school.
They were quarantined at home with their families,
pets, assorted electronic devices and Netflix.
What *were* they to do?

First, they cooked all the food in their freezer,
including, in some cases, items hoarded since Y2K.
When they ran out of freezer dinners, they foraged in the
pantry to create culinary surprises from lima beans and jello.

They cleaned their overflowing closets and drawers,
unearthing treasures, taxes from 1980 – 2019, and junk.
The trash and re-cycle workers left them hate mail,
but they kept right on pillaging and purging.

About week six, they emerged to discover SPRING with
bright, clear skies and no scent of exhaust fumes.
Bird song filled the air, daffodils danced on strong legs,
and the deer in the back yard had stopped coughing.

The people of the land were so delighted, they
volunteered to stay indoors a few more weeks --
in exchange for toilet paper.

The POET'S DOMAIN

Acknowledges

The poem Fixing It by Vanessa Jones

as being selected as the

favored or best poem
by a majority of votes
from contributors to volume 34

Thank you to all who participate by their votes for
the Poet's Domain Contributor's Prize. The
winner will receive a cash award and certificate, and
will join the ranks of future winners of same...

Meet the Poets of vol.34 ...

Contact Points, Biographies, "Bios", Pointers, Accomplishments, Publications, Favorites, Discussion Points...

S.A. Borders-Shoemaker is a poet and fantasy and science-fiction author based in the Hampton Roads region of Virginia. She has two micronovels, <u>The Conscious Objection</u>, and <u>Rooted In Time</u>, along with numerous op-eds and a number of academic articles and nonfiction narratives. She recently earned her Ph.D. Her professional work as a Conflict Resolution practitioner specializes in interpersonal communication surrounding difficult subjects. When she's not writing, she spends her time with Tim, her husband, and their audacious corgi, Edmund.

Lorraine Benedetto
My philosophy as biography:

There is something magical in
words - not just in their meanings
and connotations, but in the melodic
vibrations that can be produced by way
of things like assonance and meter.

I have long recognized that artistry
is expressed in a myriad of ways. For
me, poetry is the crafting of music -
for/by the 'pitch impaired'.

This is what has called me to a lifetime
(50+ years) of being a poet - evocative
words and subtle resonance dancing
across the page.

Joan Ellen Casey worked as an editor for New York publishers, trekked through South America alone as a female of twenty-five, raised a family, earned a doctorate from William & Mary, and wrote educational materials – then she quit to write poetry.
"The first poem I submitted for consideration won the Metrorail Public Art Project Award from the Poetry Society of Virginia. Since then I have been published in the last five volumes of *The Poet's Domain,* two other anthologies: *Distant Horizons* and *Captured*

Moments, and have contributed to the Poetry Society of Virginia's Newsletter."

Norma Cofresi is a Clinical Psychologist, a Psychoanalyst, and writer. She was born in NYC to Puerto Rican parents and lived in New York City, Puerto Rico, and Cleveland, Ohio. She is happily married, has three adult children, and two grandchildren. Norma traded an apartment in the Bronx for a home in Williamsburg, Va. where she can sit in her backyard to commune with nature. She was reborn as a poet and fiction writer a year ago when she took a creative writing class with Janice Hoffman at Thomas Nelson Community College. Members of the James City County Poets Group provide guidance, friendship, and inspiration, for which she is grateful.
You can email her at Geminiris@icloud.com

Sharon Canfield Dorsey has published fiction, non-fiction, juvenile fiction and poetry in magazines, newspapers, journals and anthologies. She is a member of National League of American Pen Women, Inc., and the James City Poets. She has received awards from Christopher Newport University Writer's Conference, Poetry Society of Virginia, Gulf Coast Writer's Association, and Chesapeake Bay Writers. She was a winner of the Art Lit Project, which displayed her poetry on the sidewalks of the city of Williamsburg, VA. Sharon is author of four children's books, *Herman, the Hermit Crab and the Mystery of the Big, Black, Shiny Thing; Revolt of the Teacups; Buddy and Ballerina Save the Library; Buddy the Bookworm Rescues the Doomed Books;* a book of poetry, *Tapestry;* a memoir, *Daughter of the Mountains,* and a travel memoir, *Road Trip.* Her poems are also included in an anthology, *Captured Moments.*

Anne Emerson is incorrigibly interested in everything, including other cultures and peoples. She likes to work with her hands, and also spends hours in thought - ideas running off in many directions. She has been active in several hobbies over the years, including writing poetry, taking photographs, gardening, sewing, knitting and crochet, and attempting to play the guitar.

She was born and raised in England. She immigrated to the U.S. with her DC-born husband on 7-7-77. They lived in the DC area for forty-one years, and retired to Williamsburg, Virginia in 2018. Anne once worked as a photographer for Sears Portrait Studio, and has taught French to young children and Economics to MBA students. Anne's poems have been published in NoVA Bards, and the Poet's Domain, in recent years. She has presented poetry (her own and others') to senior communities in Reston and Williamsburg. Anne's address for any correspondence, is: PO Box 2623, Williamsburg, Virginia 23187.

Carolyn kreiter-foronda, Virginia Poet Laureate Emerita, has co-Edited three anthologies and published nine books, including *These Flecks of Color: New and Selected Poems* and *The Embrace*, winner of the Art in Literature: The Mary Lynn Kotz Award. Her poems appear widely throughout the United States and abroad in such journals as *Nimrod, Prairie Schooner, Poet Lore, World Poetry Yearbook, Universal Oneness,* and *Best Of Literary Journals.* [www.carolynforonda.com]

Serena Fusek lives in Newport News with her husband where she is known as a somewhat eccentric cat lady. She has two full length collections of poetry: *Alphabet of Foxes* (San Francisco Bay Press) and *Ancient Maps and a Tarot Pack* which won the 2018 Bitter Oleander Press Library of Poetry Award. (She almost bought a Maine Coon Cat with the money but adopted a rescue tabby instead.) She teaches poetry at CNU's Life Long Learning Society and conducts workshops on various topics of poetic interest. Her hobby is amateur photography.

Doris Gwaltney is the author of four novels, Homefront, Shakespeare's Sister, Duncan Browdie, Gent., and Treason's Daughter.. She has also written two books of performance monologues which have been performed in many venues. She has had poetry and short fiction included in *The Greensboro Review, In Good Company, William and Mary Review,* The Poet's Domain, *Virginia Adversaria,* and other places.

G. Barry was born April 27, 1965 in Rochester, New York. When he was five years old his family moved to the nearby town of Victor where he graduated from Victor Senior High School in 1983. He earned his Bachelor's Degree from S.U.N.Y at Geneseo in upstate, New York and later received a second degree with honors in Mortuary Science from Gupton-Jones College of Mortuary Science in Atlanta, Georgia. He currently lives with his wife and family in Poquoson, Virginia where he works as a Licensed Funeral Director. His passion for writing and poetry has been a part of his life since his early years and he is a self-proclaimed old soul who enjoys delving into the deeper side of who we are as people and spiritual beings. Reflections Of An Old Soul I, II and III are the first completed anthologies in a series of recent pursuits including a series of children's books and novels still wet with ink.

Jan Hoffman holds degrees from Indiana University, teaches writing at the post-secondary level, and is published in the US and Canada. Her work appears in various literary journals and state poetry society anthologies, and she edits *A Common Wealth of Poetry* for the Poetry Society of Virginia. Her poetry collection *Soul Cookies* was released by High Tide Publications (2019), followed by her children's books *Four Fairy Friends* and *Cuatro Amigas Hadas* (2019, 2020). The Indiana Arts Commission selected three of her poems to include in its inaugural poetry archive in 2020. Jan resides in Williamsburg with her husband and two labs. She can be reached at janhoffpoetry@gmail.com and on Facebook at janhoffpoetry.

Etta Johnson is a poet, teacher, artist, writer and family matriarch.

Vanessa Jones is a middle and high school drama and English teacher. She earned her B.A. from Bucknell University where her honor's thesis was a collection of original poetry. She earned her M.A. from the University of Iowa where she began to explore the art of personal narrative. She won third place for nonfiction writing at the annual writer's conference at Christopher Newport University in 2017. Ms. Jones has written a collection of poems about raising her son, and she enjoys teaching poetry to her middle and high school students.

She is currently working on a book for adults with ADHD that combines research, personal narrative, and yes, poetry.

Terra Leigh is a poet, editor, and singer from Chesapeake, Va. She received her Bachelor's of Arts in English- Creative Writing from Virginia Tech, where she won the Stegler Poetry Prize. Then, she continued pursuing her love for writing and earned her Master's of Fine Arts in Poetry from Drew University, inspired by artists such as Maya Angelou and G Yamazawa. She has two poetry collections available, *"Ignite"* (2018) and *"So Far Away"* (2019), both published by Wider Perspectives Publishing. Outside of writing, reading, and editing, she loves to sing with her church's worship team and take sabre fencing lessons. If you're lucky, she might even speak a bit of Japanese to you, which she has been learning since 2011.

Edward W. Lull grew up in Upstate New York, and graduated from the U.S. Naval Academy in 1955. He earned a masters degree from The George Washington University in 1969. After retiring from the Navy in 1975, Lull held management and executive positions in several small hi-tech firms. He began writing poetry in retirement and has published 6 books of his poetry; he has also served four terms as President of The Poetry Society of Va.

Crickyt J. Expression Writing tools in her left hand so familiar that it feels naked without one, crayons the earliest favored, Crickyt has whispered to paper like it was a best friend all her life. In 2012, she stepped into the light of Hampton Roads open mics after a long stint of life in shadows. Finding a home and family at Norfolk's Venue on 35th, this Baltimore native was soon dubbed Little Mighty. Understanding one's voice is their most valuable asset, she uses her talents to encourage, comfort, and uplift others. Such is the focus of her new book Dear Broken Woman: Trials to Triumph.

Linda Partee As a California youngster, she wrote about everything she mused about, though never saved one scrap. Instead, her words were pushed through a hole in the wall that had been formed by too many hits of a doorknob and she's always wondered if her scraps were ever found.

Linda earned her college degrees at California State University, Fullerton; a B.A. in Communications and her M.A. in Speech & Language Pathology. During a 3-decade career in education and administration, she was called upon to focus her writing skills toward technical, educational and government requirements. The joy of words began to dissolve. In retirement, she moved cross-country to Williamsburg, enrolled in her first Christopher Wren writing class, and lovely words came flooding back. This time, she saved them. Linda began to dabble with poetry, and really likes to write in form. She is a member of the James City Poets, The Williamsburg Poetry Guild and Chesapeake Bay Writers. During the coldest months, you can find her teaching poetry through the Osher Lifelong Learning Institute at the College of William and Mary.

Dawn Riddle, a Virginia native, was born along with her identical twin in 1967. She earned degrees in Sociology at Virginia colleges: Mary Washington and William & Mary, respectively. Riddle has managed the restored Victorian 1889 *Mansion on Main* in Smithfield's Historic District for over 15 years. She leads the *Isle of Wight Writers Group* with its beloved matriarch, Doris Gwaltney. Multiple poems have been exhibited at Smithfield's Arts Center/"Arts@319" with co-sponsored themed events. Riddle has been published in recent editions of *The Poet's Domain* by Live Wire Press.

Ann Shalaski was born and raised in Connecticut and spent her formative years nurtured by a warm, loving and, at times, loud Italian family. Much of her work delves into those vivid memories. She is an award-winning poet whose pieces have appeared in numerous journals and anthologies. Her story of a family's disconnect and rivalry appears in Keeper of the Stories, a Guide to Writing Family Stories. She is the author of three poetry collections, the last of which was Just So You Know from Live Wire Press. Ann is a member of National League of American Pen Women. She is a former officer with the Poetry Society of Virginia. She hosts a monthly poetry open mic in Newport News.

Barbara Drucker Smith is a regional and national anthologized poet, non-fiction and fiction writer. She is author of <u>Darling Lorraine, the story of A. Louis Drucker, A Grateful Jewish Immigrant – Poetic Journey</u>, nominated for the Library of Virginia Awards. She is owner-operator of Louraine Publishing. She is a certified English, Speech, & Journalism teacher and taught at Ferguson High School. She's a member of Tidewater Writer's Assoc., VA Writers, Poetry Society of VA, SHARP Society of Historians, and has worked in blown glass, composing and piano, swimming and travelling the world.

Julia Travers is a writer, artist and art teacher in Central Virginia, U.S. She grew up near the Chesapeake Bay. She writes poetry, fiction, essays and news. Her creative works are published with *Heron Tree Poetry Journal, The Journal of Wild Culture, Ecological Citizen, On Being, The Mindfulness Bell,* and others. See more: juliatravers.journoportfolio.com, Twitter @traversjul.

Jack Underhill has a PhD. From George Mason University in public policy and an MA in public administration from Harvard's Kennedy School of Government along with degrees from UC Berkeley and Columbia. He retired in 1997 after forty-two years in Federal service. He participates in the poetry workshop at GMU's Osher Lifelong Learning Center, in the PSV as a former VP, and in previous volumes of <u>The Poet's Domain</u>.

J. Scott Wilson is an opaque surfaced, three-dimensional being who participates in heterotrophoism, heterosexuality and heterodontia. He has been published in <u>The Poet's Domain</u> and then helped to create the Hampton Roads Artistic Collective and Wider Perspectives Publishing. Much of his poetry expresses concern over social justice and how we, as humans, treat each other. He invites discussion at any of the many open mics he goes to all around Virginia, where he takes the stage under the name "TEECH!"

Gus M. Woodward II is a loving old soul with a young spirit born and raised in Virginia Beach. A 31 year old father and just getting started on discovering his purpose; To spread unconditional love through any and every method or medium, any interaction or conversation. He was raised by a father that taught me how to practice the art of happiness and a mother that opened up the world of creative expression at a very young age. Now as a father, his whole day rises and sets around my son. Though given a number of stage names like G2, MC Gusto, Gustarhymez he is simply Gus and poetry is his true language.

Tim Wright was born in Africa to missionary parents and has traveled the world. He is a 21 year retired United States Navy Veteran. He is a four-time *Navy Achievement Medal* and six-time *Good Conduct Medal* recipient. Since 2007, Tim has been responsible for monitoring the operational performance and quality of a national workforce development company which operates projects that help people gain and maintain meaningful, rewarding employment. He is a member of the Hampton Roads (VA) Chamber of Commerce, Tim holds a BS degree in Marketing. He is married and the proud father of three children ages 27, 22, and 15.

Rabbi Dr. Israel Zoberman is the founder and spiritual leader of Temple Lev Tikvah in Virginia Beach, Virginia. He was born in 1945 in Chu, Kazakhstan (USSR) to Polish Holocaust survivors. He spent his early childhood in Poland, Austria and Germany before moving to Israel in 1949. He came to Chicago in 1966.His poetry and translations from Hebrew have been published in *CCAR Journal, Poetica, The Jewish Spectator, The American Rabbi, Moment*, and The Poet's Domain, Volumes 5 through 34.

colophon (heavily modified)
Brought to you by Wider Perspectives Publishing, care of James
Wilson, with the mission of advancing the poetry and creative
community of Hampton Roads, Virginia.
See our production of works from ...

Patsy Bickerstaff
Edith Blake
Tanya Cunningham-Jones
    (Scientific Eve)
Terra Leigh
Ray Simmons
S.A.Borders-Shoemaker
Taz Weysweete'
Bobby K.
    (The Poor Man's Poet)
J. Scott Wilson (TEECH!)
Charles Wilson
Gloria Darlene Mann
Neil Spirtas
Zach Crowe
Jorge Mendez & JT Williams
Sarah Eileen Williams
Stephanie Diana (Noftz)

the Hampton Roads
    Artistic Collective
Jason Brown (Drk Mtr)
Martina Champion
Tony Broadway
Ken Sutton
Crickyt J. Expression
Lisa M. Kendrick
Cassandra IsFree
Nich (Nicholis Williams)
Samantha Geovjian Clarke
Natalie Morison-Uzzle
Gus Woodward II
Chichi Iwuori
Catherine TL Hodges
Jack Cassada
Kent Knowlton

... and others to come soon.

These authors, along with contributors to Poet's Domain represent
the fertile soil of creativity. Somewhere among these names are voices
ready to grow into the literary garden of the near future. Seek them out at the
open mics and book shelves in your area, or find them online – somewhere
herein are the words you or someone you know need in your lives.

Need suggestion or publication of your own work...

    HRACandWPP@outlook.com

Made in the USA
Middletown, DE
19 February 2021

34035803R00096